STEP BY STEP

INTELLIGENCE TESTS

by

C. N. BISSENDEN

Nelson

Thomas Nelson and Sons Ltd
Nelson House Mayfield Road
Walton-on-Thames Surrey
KT12 5PL UK

51 York Place
Edinburgh
EH1 3JD UK

Thomas Nelson (Hong Kong) Ltd
Toppan Building 10/F
22A Westlands Road
Quarry Bay Hong Kong

Thomas Nelson Australia
102 Dodds Street
South Melbourne
Victoria 3205
Australia

Nelson Canada
1120 Birchmount Road
Scarborough Ontario
M1K 5G4 Canada

First published by E J Arnold and Son Ltd 1958
ISBN 0-08-008251-3

A Teacher's Book is available: ISBN 0-08-008252-1

This edition published by Thomas Nelson and Sons Ltd 1990
ISBN 0-17-410294-1
NPN 9 8 7 6 5 4 3

Printed in Hong Kong

NOTES

This book contains exercises which are original in design or are based on standard types of questions set in a large number of Intelligence Tests.

The exercises are graded to give gradual improvement with a wide age-range of children. Even if children do not do Intelligence Tests for their school assessment, they will get enjoyment by working the exercises, and an opportunity to improve their mental capacity.

The exercises give examples of different methods of answering questions—underlining, ringing, deletions, etc.

CONTENTS

EXERCISE 1

You will see that each row of numbers or letters goes along in steps. Sometimes there are capital letters and sometimes small letters, and sometimes numbers and letters. You must take care to put in the right kind of letters. Here is the alphabet to help you:—

A B C D E F G H I J K L M N O P Q R S T U V W X Y Z

1.	A	B	C	D	E	......
2.	1	2	3	4	5	......
3.	G	H	I	J	K	......
4.	7	8	9	10	11	......
5.	r	s	t	u	v	......
6.	Z	Y	X	W	V	......
7.	O	N	M	L	K	......
8.	9	8	7	6	5	......
9.	O	P	......	R	S	T
10.	8	9	10	......	12	13
11.	Y	X	W	V	......	T
12.	m	......	o	p	q	r
13.	21	22	......	24	25	26
14.	31	30	29	28	......	26
15.	1A	2B	3C	4D	......	6F
16.	Kk	Ll	Mm	Nn	Oo	......
17.	7Q	8R	9S	10T	......	12V
18.	1Z	2Y	3X	4W	5V	......
19.	AaA	BbB	CcC	DdD	......	FfF
20.	mMm	......	oOo	pPp	qQq	rRr

EXERCISE 2

In these questions one word has been left out. Can you put the word in? This is how it is done ;

Mother is to woman as Father is to man.

The word man has been put in because mother is a woman and father is a man.

1. Cat is to Kitten as Dog is to ....
2. Sheep is to Baa as Cow is to ....
3. Ear is to Hear as Eye is to ....
4. Mary is to Girl as John is to ....
5. Red is to Stop as Green is to ....
6. Foot is to Leg as Hand is to ....
7. Horse is to Stable as Pig is to ....
8. Tongue is to Taste as Nose is to ....
9. Yes is to No as In is to ....
10. Girl is to Boy as Woman is to ....
11. Milk is to Drink as Cake is to ....
12. Up is to .... as Come is to Go.
13. Sad is to .... as Happy is to Laugh.
14. Table is to .... as Stove is to Iron.
15. Gate is to Garden as .... is to House.
16. Grass is to .... as Poppy is to Red.
17. .... is to Sheep as Calf is to Cow.
18. Man is to Walk as Bird is to ....
19. Stand is to Up as Sit is to ....
20. Sheep is to .... as Cow is to Hair.

EXERCISE 3

Now look at these lines of words. In each line there is one word which should not be there. It is not in the same group as the other words in the line. Cross out the word. Like this :

Cow Dog Pig ~~Man~~ Cat.

You will see why MAN is crossed out.

1. Cup Plate Can Jug Basin Dish
2. Jim Mary Dick Joe Sam Mick
3. Apple Pear Orange Plum Carrot
4. Pencil Pen Ruler Crayon Chalk
5. Tea Milk Oil Coffee Cocoa
6. Car Table Chair Bed Sideboard
7. Swan Canary Sparrow Spider Crow
8. Oak Weed Ash Elm Poplar
9. Coat Hat Bonnet Arm Shoe
10. Red Blue Stop Yellow Green
11. Eye Arm Hand Glasses Mouth
12. Roof Door Road Window Floor
13. Pup Kitten Calf Baby Man
14. Desk Chair Piano Bus Table
15. Sleep Breakfast Dinner Tea Lunch
16. Boy Girl Child Baby Pram
17. Meat Peas Beans Cabbages Potatoes
18. Crawl Baby Walk Run Gallop
19. Cake Bread Biscuits Toast Drink
20. Toe Foot Shoe Leg Knee

EXERCISE 4

Here is a new kind of question. If you underline one part of the words in the brackets you will have a true sentence. This is how it is done :—

A dog always has (<u>skin</u>; a kennel ; a master)

1. A classroom always has (a door ; paper ; maps)
2. A boy always has (a tie ; black hair ; a mouth)
3. A car always has (four seats ; wheels ; a red body)
4. A lady always has (a hat ; a head ; stockings)
5. A town always has (houses ; buses ; a castle)
6. A book always has (pages ; pictures ; a red cover)
7. A tree always has (leaves ; roots ; flowers)
8. A house always has (a garden ; furniture ; walls)
9. Rain is always (heavy ; wet ; cold)
10. A boy always (talks ; runs ; breathes)
11. A man always has (a son ; a car ; a body)
12. A horse always has (a saddle ; a cart ; a neck)
13. A bus always has (a driver ; passengers ; an engine)
14. A country always has (a king ; ships ; land)
15. A foot always has (a shoe ; a sole ; a bell)
16. Coal is always (hot ; cold ; black)
17. A cat always has (mice ; kittens ; fur)
18. A runner always has (legs ; prizes ; races)
19. Tea is always (hot ; cold ; brown)
20. George is always a (boy ; man ; name)

EXERCISE 5

This is the alphabet :

A B C D E F G H I J K L M N O P Q R S T U V W X Y Z

Can you answer these questions correctly ?

1. How many letters are there in the alphabet ? ....
2. What is the sixth letter ? ....
3. What is the 13th letter ? ....
4. What is the 24th letter ? ....
5. What is the letter which follows the 25th letter ? ....
6. What is the letter which follows the 12th letter ? ....
7. What is the letter which comes before the 7th letter ? ....
8. What is the letter which comes before the 22nd letter ? ....
9. What is the 3rd letter after the 6th letter ? ....
10. What is the 4th letter after the 17th letter ? ....
11. If you draw a line halfway along the alphabet the line is between the letters ....
12. What is the 4th letter after the halfway mark in the alphabet ? ....
13. How many capital letters in the alphabet use only curved lines ? ....
14. How many use only straight lines ? ....
15. How many use curved and straight lines ? ....
16. How many use only two straight lines ? ....
17. Make a word from the 2nd, 15th, and 23rd letters. ....
18. Make a word from the 22nd, 5th, 18th and 25th letters. ....
19. There are .... vowels in the alphabet.
20. The third vowel in the alphabet is ....

EXERCISE 6

1	2	3	4	5	6	7	8	9	10	11	12	13	14	15	16	17
A	B	C	D	E	F	G	H	I	J	K	L	M	N	O	P	Q
18	19	20	21	22	23	24	25	26								
R	S	T	U	V	W	X	Y	Z								

This is a simple form of code. Instead of writing letters in words I am going to write numbers.

Example :— 20 8 9 19   9 19   1   3 15 4 5
T H I S   I S   A   C O D E

In this example I have put under each number the letter the number stands for in the code, and then I know what the sentence is. Here is some practice for you :—

1. 3 15 13 5   2. 13 1 14 25   3. 21 19 5 6 21 12
... ...

4. 19 9 13 16 12 5   5. 3 1 20 3 8 9 14 7
... ...

6. 3 15 13 5   20 15   20 5 1
... ...

7. 4 15 7 19   5 1 20   13 5 1 20
... ...

8. 12 15 15 11   2 15 20 8   23 1 25 19
... ...

9. 2 5   3 1 18 5   6 21 12   23 8 5 14
... ...
3 18 15 19 19 9 14 7   18 15 1 4 19
... ...

10. 9   23 9 12 12   3 15 13 5   20 15   20 5 1
...   .

In the bracket at the end of the line write T if the sentence is true, or F if it is false.

11. 3 1 20 19   5 1 20   13 9 3 5   ( )
... ...

12. 23 5   12 9 22 5   9 14   20 18 5 5 19   ( )
... ...

13. 18 15 19 5 19 7 18 15 23 9 14

... ...

7 1 18 4 5 14 19

... ... ( )

14. 13 5 14 1 12 23 1 25 19 23 5 1 18

... ...

8 1 20 19

... ... ( )

15. 1 12 12 20 18 5 5 19 8 1 22 5

... ...

18 15 15 20 19

... ... ( )

In each of these sentences three letters are missing. Put in the brackets the numbers which should be in the spaces.

16. 1 4 ( ) 7 8 ( ) 19 12 5 ( ) 19

... ...

17. 2 ( ) 25 19 12 ( ) 11 5

... ...

19 23 ( ) 5 20 19

... ...

18. 9 19 5 5 23 ( ) 20 8 13 ( )

... ...

5 ( ) 5 19

... ...

19. 20 8 5 19 ( ) 14 19 8 ( ) 14 5 19

... ...

2 25 ( ) 1 25

... ...

20. 4 15 14 ( ) 20 20 ( ) 18 15 23

... ...

12 ( ) 20 20 5 18 1 2 15 21 20

... ...

EXERCISE 7

You should put a cross in front of what you think is the best reason. Like this :—

We wear coats in winter because
- (a) coats are smart.
- (b) coats button up the front.
- X (c) we must keep ourselves warm.

1. We use soap to wash our hands because
   - (a) soap sometimes smells nice.
   - (b) it gets them clean more easily.
   - (c) it is a pretty colour.
2. We put our litter into baskets because
   - (a) we want to keep everywhere tidy.
   - (b) we cannot put litter in our pockets.
   - (c) litter may be clean paper.
3. We look both ways before we cross the road because
   - (a) we want to get home quickly.
   - (b) cars and lorries can come both ways.
   - (c) we might see our friend across the road.
4. We wear wellington boots in wet weather because
   - (a) they are made of rubber.
   - (b) they keep our feet dry.
   - (c) they are black.
5. We must take care of our teeth because
   - (a) they are white.
   - (b) they help us to eat our food properly.
   - (c) they are in our mouths.
6. We say 'Thank You' for a present because
   - (a) we are polite.
   - (b) we like to receive presents.
   - (c) we like unfastening the parcel.
7. We are kind to our pets because
   - (a) otherwise pets might bite us.
   - (b) they know we will care for them.
   - (c) they eat meat.
8. Flowers are pretty because
   - (a) they grow in soil.
   - (b) they have stalks and leaves.
   - (c) they have different colours and shapes
9. We read books because
   - (a) we don't like playing games.
   - (b) we like the stories in books.
   - (c) we have two eyes.
10. Workmen dig holes in the road.
    - (a) for children to fall into.
    - (b) to get soil for their gardens.
    - (c) to repair pipes and cables.

EXERCISE 8

In each sentence cross out the part of a word which spoils the sense of it.

1. Mother laid the stable and we had tea.
2. I read a good brook last week.
3. The scar went quickly along the street.
4. He bought a toy which was very cheaper.
5. I play with a fresh story every day.
6. The wind began to below hard.
7. The lady fell and hurt his leg.
8. The ship sailed far across the seaside.
9. He bought it fort a pound.
10. The boy wore a blue and red tile.
11. He was out in the train and got wet.
12. Mary said it was there coat.
13. The coat was dripped from top to bottom.
14. Every boy should story his hardest.
15. She was a big glass for her age.
16. The baby was fast asleep in the scout.
17. I like petals for my dinner.
18. The plane took coffee for Paris.
19. The graceful was won by the fastest boy.
20. Too many cuphooks spoil the broth.

EXERCISE 9

In this exercise underline the two parts of words on the right which combine to make the word at the beginning of each line.

Like this:—

LION—NO ON IO LO LI

You will see that the two parts which I have underlined make up the word LION.

1.	BOOK	—	BO	OO	KO	BOO	OK
2.	CHAIR	—	CH	AI	IR	CHA	HA
3.	TABLE	—	TAB	BLE	AB	LE	TABL
4.	FIRE	—	IR	RE	FI	FIR	IRE
5.	DOOR	—	OO	OR	OD	DO	RO
6.	BREAD	—	EA	ED	BR	BRE	EAD
7.	JELLY	—	JEL	LLY	JE	ELY	ELL
8.	PUPPY	—	PPY	UPP	PUPY	PY	PU
9.	GLASS	—	SS	GL	LAS	ASS	AS
10.	PIPES	—	PES	PI	IPE	ES	SEP
11.	LEAVE	—	EA	EV	LE	AV	AVE
12.	PIECE	—	IEC	PIE	ECE	CE	EC
13.	STAMP	—	AMP	TAM	MP	ST	PA

In the next lines draw a ring round the two parts of words which are not needed to make the first word. Like this:— COCOA — CO CO OA AC A

STABLE — LE BA AB TA ST

14.	SPREAD	—	ER	RE	AD	PR	SP
15.	FOLDER	—	DL	LD	OL	ER	FO
16.	TINKLE	—	LE	KL	TI	NK	IN
17.	PRINTS	—	NT	TS	IN	RI	PR
18.	THUMBS	—	MBS	HU	BS	TH	UM
19.	STREAM	—	ST	AE	RE	MA	AM
20.	WAITER	—	IT	ER	WA	TE	AI

EXERCISE 10

Put these parts of sentences in their correct order, so that they follow on as they should do. Put the number 1 in front of the first, number 2 in front of the second, and so on.

1.	John	( )	went to bed
		( )	had his supper
		( )	woke up
		( )	had his breakfast
		( )	went to sleep
2.	The farmer	( )	sowed his wheat
		( )	cut the corn
		( )	ploughed the field
		( )	gathered the corn
		( )	weeded the young corn
3.	Mother	( )	made the mixture
		( )	baked the cake
		( )	bought some flour
		( )	put it in the oven
		( )	gave me a slice
4.	The man	( )	got out of bed
		( )	went to work
		( )	put on his coat
		( )	put on his shirt
		( )	put on his vest
5.	The boy	( )	learned to cry
		( )	went to school
		( )	learned to stand
		( )	learned to walk
		( )	learned to crawl
6.	The driver	( )	got into the car
		( )	drove away
		( )	opened the car door
		( )	closed the door
		( )	started the engine
7.	At Christmas we	( )	sent our Christmas cards
		( )	wrote our 'Thank You' letters
		( )	woke up on Christmas morning
		( )	showed everyone our presents
		( )	opened our parcels

EXERCISE 11

If you know the four main points of the compass (North, South, East and West) you should be able to answer these questions. In all these questions you should remember that North is always straight up the page.

Here are nine towns represented by dots arranged on the page. Look carefully at them and then answer the questions.

Ashton •	Belton •	Cayton •
Delton •	Elton •	Fulton •
Gorton •	Hilton •	Lowton •

1. How many towns are North of Lowton ....
2. How many towns are West of Elton ....
3. How many towns are East of Delton ....
4. How many towns are South of Belton ....
5. Fulton is .... of Lowton.
6. Delton is .... of Gorton.
7. Hilton is .... of Lowton.
8. Elton is .... of Delton.
9. Hilton is .... of Lowton and .... of Gorton.
10. Elton is .... of Belton and .... of Hilton.
11. Cayton is .... of Fulton and .... of Belton.
12. Belton is .... of Elton and Hilton and .... of Cayton.
13. .... has no town North or East of it.
14. .... has no town South or West of it.
15. .... has no town North or West of it.
16. .... is the only town with another town North, South, East and West of it.
17. .... is the only town with another town in each direction except the East.
18. .... is the only town with another town to the North, West and East, but no town to the South.
19. I travel North from Elton to ...., then turn to the............ to Cayton.
20. If I live at Cayton, Fulton is then .... of me, and Ashton is to the ....

EXERCISE 12

This exercise is all about odd numbers and even numbers. Put the letter O under the number if it is an odd number or the letter E if it is an even number.

Like this :—	3	8	15	19	26
	O	E	O	O	E

1.	7	12	16	23	28
	...	...	...	...	...
2.	36	48	59	62	74
	...	...	...	...	...
3.	101	147	226	718	50
	...	...	...	...	...

4. Using the figures 2, 1, 4 make an odd number..........................
5. Using the figures 0, 1, 3, make an even number ....
6. How many must you add to 57 to make it an even number ? ......
7. What is the next even number after 33 ? ....
8. How many odd numbers are there between 10 and 20 ? ....
9. What is the next number above 75 which can be written with <u>two</u> even number figures ? Do not count 0 as an even number. ....
10. If I write the numbers from 24 to 42, how many times must I write the figure 3 ? ....

Here is a list of numbers. Try to answer the questions which follow and put your answer in the brackets after the numbers.

24682 ( )	31211 ( )	82714 ( )	11210 ( )
13206 ( )	51515 ( )	11213 ( )	31213 ( )
10306 ( )	13579 ( )	44144 ( )	

11. Put the letter E against the number containing all even numbers.
12. Put B against the two numbers which contain the same figures but in a different order.
13. Put L against the largest number.
14. Put S against the smallest number.
15. Put T against the number containing the most 3s.
16. Put X against the number which will divide by 10.
17. Put O against the number which contains all odd numbers.
18. Put P against the number which will divide by 3.
19. Put H against the number which begins and ends with the same two double numbers.
20. Put R against the number which has the same figure at each end and in the middle.

EXERCISE 13

Here are some puzzles for you. Read carefully what is written and then answer the questions.

1. Mary and Joan like skipping.
   Ann and Mary wear glasses.

   Who might break her glasses while she is skipping ? ....

2. Jack and John like sweets.
   Joe and John are untidy.

   Who was the boy who dropped his toffee paper in the street ?..............

3. Jane and Jim like dogs.
   Elsie and Bill like horses.
   Jane and Elsie are tall.

   Who was the tall girl I saw out riding ? ....

4. In our street there are gardens.
   Mr. Brown and Mr. Green grow roses.
   Mr. Green and Mr. Smith grow lupins.
   Mr. Smith and Mr. Brown grow daisies.

   I saw Mr. .... picking roses and daisies in his garden.

   Mr. .... gave me lupins and roses from his garden.

   Mrs. .... has a vase full of daisies and lupins from her husband's garden.

5. Mary and June are neat writers.
   June and Sally do sums well.
   Mary and Sally are sisters.

   Which girl do you think will be top of the class ? ....

6. Jim is taller than Jack.
   Harry is taller than Jim.

   Who is the smallest ? .... Who is the tallest ? ....

7. Lowtown is bigger than Newtown.
   Downtown is bigger than Lowtown.

   Which town is the biggest ? ....

EXERCISE 14

Here are some more letters and figures going along in steps but this time you should draw a ring round the one that does not fit into the steps. There is only one mistake in each line. Here is the alphabet to help you.

A B C D E F G H I J K L M N O P Q R S T U V W X Y Z

1.	A	B	C	D	E	G
2.	1	3	4	5	6	7
3.	Z	Y	S	W	V	U
4.	12	13	10	9	8	7
5.	r	s	T	u	v	w
6.	2	4	6	7	10	12
7.	A	b	c	d	e	f
8.	21	20	19	15	17	16
9.	aB	aC	aD	aE	aF	ag
10.	M1	N2	O0	P4	Q5	R6
11.	1	3	5	7	9	10
12.	BbB	CCC	DdD	EeE	FfF	GgG
13.	0A	0B	0C	0d	0E	0F
14.	1	2	3	4	3	6
15.	8	9	10	11	21	13
16.	1.	2.	3,	4.	5.	6.
17.	UA	UB	Uc	UD	UE	UF
18.	A;	A:	A:	A:	A:	A:
19.	21	31	41	51	61	81
20.	A7	B8	C9	D01	E11	F12

EXERCISE 15

In each line one word has been left out. Can you put it in ? You have done some of these puzzles before.

1. Boy is to Girl as Father is to ....
2. Fire is to Warmth as Lamp is to ....
3. Light is to Heavy as Dark is to ....
4. Pencil is to Draw as Pen is to ....
5. Up is to High as Down is to ....
6. Water is to Bread as .... is to Eat.
7. Table is to Wood as Window is to ....
8. Sing is to Bird as .... is to Pig.
9. Here is to Place as When is to ....
10. Arrive is to Come as Depart is to ....
11. Oak is to Tree as Horse is to ....
12. Like is to Love as Dislike is to ....
13. Steam is to Railway Engine as .... is to Car.
14. .... is to Aeroplane as Driver is to Car.

In the next lines you should cross out the word in the brackets that you do not need.

15. Up is to Down as Top is to (Spin, Bottom)
16. Ball is to Rubber as Table is to (Wood, Flat)
17. Eye is to See as Tooth is to (Bite, Ache)
18. Baby is to Milk as Bird is to (Nest, Worm)
19. Horse is to Stable as Dog is to (Puppy, Kennel)
20. Red is to Danger as Green is to (Grass, Safety).

EXERCISE 16

One word in each line tells you what all the other words in the line are. This is called the ' GROUP ' word. Draw a line under each group word. Like this :—

Cow Dog Pig <u>Animal</u> Sheep.

1. Meat Bread Food Cake Jam
2. Crow Bird Lark Wren Robin
3. Number One Two Three Six
4. Red Blue Yellow Colour Green
5. Pear Apple Plum Fruit Banana
6. Mary Name Jane Jack George
7. Coat Hat Clothes Dress Jersey
8. Oak Tree Elm Ash Poplar
9. Tin Metal Brass Iron Lead
10. Monday Day Tuesday Wednesday Sunday
11. Pansy Rose Flower Daffodil Snowdrop
12. Father Postman Tailor Men Cobbler
13. Weather Foggy Snowing Raining Freezing
14. Milk Tea Drinks Coffee Cocoa
15. Bricklayer Tailor Workman Baker Engineer
16. Month April May June July
17. Food Cheese Bread Cake Porridge
18. Sea Pond Lake Water Pool
19. Trawlers Liners Ships Ferry-boats Tramp-steamers
20. Hammer File Screwdriver Tool Plane

EXERCISE 17

You have done some questions like these before. On this page you should underline two words in the brackets which will make a true sentence. Like this :—

A tree always has (leaves, flowers, trunk, roots)

1. A baby always has (curls, body, teeth, lips)
2. A flower always has (a stalk, scent, leaves, petals)
3. A kettle always has (water, handle, a spout, steam)
4. A field always has (grass, corn, soil, stones)
5. A school always has (walls, a bell, doors, boys)
6. A stocking always has (a foot, a hole, wool, a leg)
7. A face always has (skin, a mouth, colour, whiskers)
8. A woman always has (a baby, a husband, a name, a head)
9. A house always has (a clock, walls, a carpet, a window)
10. A room always has a (floor, door, picture, clock)
11. A door always has (hinges, a handle, a knocker, a letter-box)
12. A bicycle always has a (wheel, frame, light, rider)
13. An oak tree always has (branches, acorns, leaves, bark)
14. A shoe always has (a sole, leather, rubber, a heel)
15. A mother has (a son, a daughter, a child, a baby)
16. A mirror always has a (shape, frame, hook, glass)
17. A son has a (father, sister, mother, brother)
18. A daughter has (parents, children, presents, a name)
19. A box always has a (lid, bottom, side, wood)
20. A day always has (light, sunshine, hours, rain)

EXERCISE 18

Here is the alphabet :—

A B C D E F G H I J K L M N O P Q R S T U V W X Y Z

1. If F comes before J write Y for ' Yes '. If it does not, write N for ' No '. ......
2. If L comes before Y write Y. If it doesn't, write N. ......
3. If P comes before O, write Y. If it doesn't, write N. ......
4. If S comes before B, write S. If it doesn't, write B. ......
5. If P comes before L, write Z. If it doesn't write A. ......
6. If N comes before K, draw a circle. If it doesn't, draw a square. ......
7. If S comes before M, draw a circle in a square. If it doesn't, draw a square by itself. ......
8. If J comes before both P and U, write RIGHT. If it doesn't, write WRITE. ....
9. If K comes before both E and O, write YES. If it doesn't, write NO. ......
10. If F is the the same number of letters from the beginning as U is from the end, write YES. If it isn't, write NO. ....
11. There are five letters together in the alphabet with curved shapes. Which is the middle one ? ....
12. There are five letters together with only straight line shapes. Which is the middle one ? ....
13. What is the letter which is the same number of letters from the end of the alphabet as E is from the beginning ? ....
14. What word can be made by using the 9th, 4th, and 12th letters of the alphabet ? ....
15. If the first four letters of the alphabet were put after Z, what would be the 4th letter of the new alphabet ? ....
16. What are the letters of the alphabet which need four straight strokes to make each one of them ? ....
17. What letter is in all these words ?
    DONE DANE DOLL LEAD ....
18. What letter is in all these words ?
    PIECE PAINT PLIERS LIKES ....
19. What letters are in all these words ?
    DINNER PENNY CERTAIN NEARLY ....
20. What is the first letter in the alphabet which I can add to STO to make a word ? ....

EXERCISE 19

In these questions numbers are used instead of letters.
Example :—If 123 stands for BAT what does 321 stand for ? (TAB)

You will see that 3 stands for T because it is the last figure in the number representing BAT. 2 is the second figure in the number representing BAT and so it stands for A. 1 is the first figure in the number representing BAT and so it is B. That makes 321 stand for TAB.

Now try these—

1. If 456 stands for PAN, what is 654 ? ....
2. If 259 stands for SAW, what is 952 ? ....
3. If 516 stands for BIN, what is 615 ? ....
4. If 237 stands for BEN, what is 2337 ? ....
5. If 1258 stands for LANE, what is 1825 ? ....
6. If 2564 stands for LEAP, what is 4625 ? ....
7. If 14227 stands for TABBY, what is 2427 ? ....
8. If 34456 stands for APPLE, what is 4356 ? ....
9. If 62753 stands for AFTER, what is 2557 ? ....
10. If 736626 stands for TERROR, what is 627736 ? ....

If 123456789 stands for HOUSEMAID, what words do the following numbers stand for :

11.	62345	....	12.	4789	....
13.	9254	....	14.	1579	....
15.	74454	....	16.	41765	....
17.	1265	....	18.	4556	....
19.	67894	....	20.	417954	....

EXERCISE 20

Which is the best reason ? Draw a ring round a, b or c.

1. We put the address on an envelope
   (a) to tell us to whom we are writing.
   (b) so that the postman will deliver it to the right person.
   (c) because we can write neatly.
2. London is the capital of England because
   (a) the Government is there.
   (b) it is on the River Thames.
   (c) it has underground trains.
3. We go to school
   (a) to improve our knowledge.
   (b) to let mother have a quiet time.
   (c) to wear our uniform.
4. People go to watch football matches
   (a) to shout at the referee.
   (b) to shout at the players.
   (c) to enjoy watching the skill of the players.
5. To tighten a nut
   (a) we use nutcrackers.
   (b) we use a spanner of the right size.
   (c) we oil it well.
6. We have legs
   (a) so that we can wear stockings.
   (b) to prevent our bodies from touching the ground.
   (c) so that we can move about.
7. Curtains are put to windows
   (a) to keep the daylight out.
   (b) to make our rooms more private.
   (c) to hide the dirty panes.
8. Iron sinks in water
   (a) because it is lighter than water.
   (b) because it is heavier than water.
   (c) because iron rusts in water.
9. We drink milk because
   (a) it is delivered in bottles.
   (b) the milkman has to make a profit.
   (c) it is nourishing.
10. Tea grows in India because
   (a) it is the only country where conditions are suitable.
   (b) the climate is suitable.
   (c) it says 'Indian Tea' on the packet.

EXERCISE 21

In these sentences two words have changed places. Draw a line under each of the two words. Like this :—

The men climbed the apples to pick trees.

Apples and trees are underlined because if those two words change places the sentence is sensible.

1. The fire lit the man in the grate.
2. Mice like cats and fresh milk.
3. My leg is at the bottom of my foot.
4. He wrote in the pencil with his book.
5. He put the table on the saucer.
6. Coats wear boys to keep them warm.
7. People like dogs to feed them.
8. We grow heads to protect our hair.
9. Write your pen with ink and fill a story.
10. Fill a hole and dig it with stones.
11. The early worm catches the bird.
12. The child lay on the milk and cried for ground.
13. The baby put the mother to bed.
14. Which grub has a pear in it?
15. Pour the dirty drain down the water.
16. The rider on the fence jumped over the horse.
17. Roads are driven on the left of the cars.
18. Paint the brush in the paint then dip the door.
19. ‘ I boy if you can ’ said the can.
20. I right with my write hand.

EXERCISE 22

Here are two lists of words. Each word in the first column is associated with one word in the second column. Put the number of the word in the first column alongside its partner in the second column.

1. Sugar	( )	ball
2. Gas	( )	rope
3. Knife	( )	butter
4. Foot	( )	basin
5. Play	( )	lumps
6. Tooth	( )	fork
7. Dairy	( )	pump
8. Skipping	( )	ground
9. Pudding	( )	ache
10. Bicycle	( )	stove

Here are another two lists of words. The words in the second column match with words in the first column, each pair having the same letters in them. Put the letter of the word in the second column behind the word in the first column.

11. NIPS	( )	a. TIME
12. PEAR	( )	b. MADE
13. MITE	( )	c. SMILE
14. SLOPE	( )	d. REAP
15. DAME	( )	e. LEAST
16. BREAD	( )	f. PINS
17. SLIME	( )	g. BARED
18. RASP	( )	h. POLES
19. STALE	( )	i. TARE
20. RATE	( )	j. SPAR

EXERCISE 23

A little girl likes threading beads in patterns. She has coloured beads, which are here shown by letters. These are the colours and sizes :—

Large White	W	Small White	w	Large Yellow	Y
Small Yellow	y	Large Blue	B	Small Blue	b
Large Red	R	Small Red	r		

1. Can you put the beads BRy in order with the large red one first and the small yellow one in the middle ? ....
2. Now put the beads WbY in order with the large yellow first and the small blue last. ....
3. Put the beads BRyw in order—Large blue first, large red after small yellow and small white after the other three beads. ....
4. Put the beads yyRR in order starting with a red and having no two of the same colour together and no two of the same size together. ....
5. Put the beads BBbbRR in order starting with a red, followed by large blue, and no two blues of the same size together. ....
6. Put the beads RRrrB in order starting with a large red and finish with a pattern that is the same backward or forward. ....
7. Put the beads RRRBBB in order starting with a large red and have no two reds together. ....
8. Put the beads BBBBWWWWY in order with every white followed by a blue with yellow as the middle bead. ....

Complete the following strings of beads in pattern, putting the correct bead where there is a dot.

9. B — R — B — R — B — R — B — R — B — R — ...— ...
10. B — W — R — B — W — R — B — W — R — B — ...— ...
11. Y — W — R — Y — W — R — Y — W — ...— Y — ...— R
12. Y — R — B — W — Y — R — B — W — Y — R — ...— ...
13. B — R — Y — B — ...— Y — B — R — ... B — ...— Y
14. W — Y — W — Y — W — Y — ...— Y — W — ...— ...— Y
15. B — b — B — b — B — b — B — b — B — b — ...— ...
16. r — R — ...— R — r — R — r — R — r — ...— r — R
17. B — b — B — b — B — ...— B — b — B — b — B — b
18. B — y — R — B — y — R — B — ...— R — ...— y — R
19. Y — w — r — B — Y — ...— ...— B — ...— w — ...— B
20. ...— ...— y — R — W — b — y — R — W — b — y — R

EXERCISE 24

Put these parts of sentences in their right order. Put figure 1 in front of the first, figure 2 in front of the second and so on. Read through each five before deciding the order.

1. To light a fire
   - ( ) lay the sticks on the paper
   - ( ) light the paper
   - ( ) get some coal, sticks and paper
   - ( ) strike a match
   - ( ) clean out the grate
2. Last winter
   - ( ) the ice broke
   - ( ) the boy was rescued
   - ( ) the boy ran on the ice
   - ( ) the boy fell through the ice
   - ( ) the pond was frozen
3. Birds
   - ( ) lay eggs
   - ( ) feed young ones
   - ( ) hatch out young ones
   - ( ) make nests
   - ( ) leave their nests
4. To sew on a button
   - ( ) put the needle through the button
   - ( ) put the needle back through the cloth
   - ( ) take a needle and thread
   - ( ) thread the needle
   - ( ) put the needle through the cloth
5. To make a cup of tea
   - ( ) pour the boiling water into the pot
   - ( ) put the tea into the teapot
   - ( ) put the kettle to boil
   - ( ) buy some tea from the shop
   - ( ) fill the kettle with water
6. The little girl was burned because
   - ( ) he forgot to fix the guard
   - ( ) it was made of cotton
   - ( ) she stood near the fire
   - ( ) her father lit the fire
   - ( ) her dress touched the flames

EXERCISE 25

To work this exercise you will need to know the eight main points of the compass.

Nine boys make a diamond pattern in the playground. Albert at the top of the group is the boy on the North side.

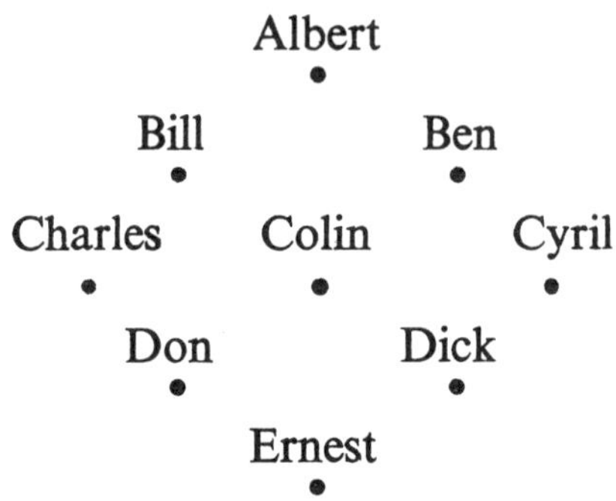

Now answer these questions. You may use abbreviations for directions where necessary.

1. Which boy is North of Colin ? ....
2. Which boy is North of Dick ? ....
3. Which boy is West of Dick ? ....
4. Which boy is East of Colin ? ....
5. .... is North-East of Bill.
6. Colin is .... of Dick.
7. Colin is South-West of ....
8. Cyril is .... of Ben.
9. How many boys are South-West of Ben ? ....

10. Colin and Cyril are .... of Charles.

11. Colin and .... are .... of Ben.

12. Charles would have to move .... to change places with Albert.

13. Albert would have to move .... to change places with Ernest.

14. Don would have to pass .... if he moved North-East to change places with ....

Bill has three ways of reaching Dick :—

15. He can go East to ...., and then .... to Dick.

16. He can go South to .... and then .... to Dick.

17. He can go South-East to .... and then .... to Dick.

18. In what directions (in their correct order) would Dick run if he runs to Ben (   ), then on to Bill (   ), then on to Don (   ) and back to his place (   ).

19. What directions will Ernest run if he runs to Cyril (   ), then on to Albert (   ) then on to Charles (   ) and back to his place (   ).

20. What directions will Don go if he runs to Dick (   ), then on to Cyril (   ), then on to Ben (   ), and back to his place (   ).

EXERCISE 26

Put a ring round the smallest number in each row.

1.	27	72	21	12	22
2.	123	132	213	231	321
3.	516	165	156	561	615
4.	217	712	127	172	271
5.	467	647	746	764	674

Look at these numbers and then answer the questions.

1 2 3 4 5 6 7 8 9 10 11 12 13 14 15 16 17 18 19 20

6. Add together all the single figure odd numbers. ....
7. Add together the two biggest even numbers. ....
8. Take the second biggest odd number from the second biggest even number. ....
9. Which number will divide by both 5 and 3 ? ....
10. Add together the lowest four odd numbers, and take the answer from the total of the highest two even numbers. ....

Underline the smallest and the biggest number in each line.

11.	3124	1234	4132	4231	4321
12.	9876	7896	6978	9786	6987
13.	2568	2586	2856	2865	2658
14.	42063	36042	24630	36024	23460
15.	64357	76543	76435	75634	73645

Now look at these numbers.

42683 ( ) 62438 ( ) 28648 ( ) 28262 ( ) 26438 ( )

16. Put Y after the number which has a figure twice in it.
17. Put L after the odd number.
18. Put H after the biggest number.
19. Put S after the lowest number.
20. Put T after the number with the same figure three times in it.

EXERCISE 27

Write in brackets at the end of each problem any number which is not needed to work the sum. Do not work the sum.

Like this ; A boy age 12 has 14 more marbles than his brother, who has 5. How many marbles has he ? (12)

The number 12 is put in the brackets because the boy's age, which is 12, is not needed to work the sum.

1. I went into the baker's shop at 10 o'clock and bought 6 cakes at 3p. each. How much did I pay the baker ? (   )

2. A man was born in 1892. How old will he be in 1959 if he has a son who was born in 1926 ? (   )

3. Potatoes are £1.25 a bag. Carrots are £1.38 a bag. What does a greengrocer pay for 5 bags of carrots? (   )

4. In a class there are 22 boys and 18 girls sitting in 21 desks. How many children are in the class ? (   )

5. In 3 days a farmer planted 35 apple trees and 42 pear trees in his orchard. How many fruit trees did he plant? (   )

6. I bought 6 lettuces at 4p each. I gave the greengrocer a 50p piece. What did the lettuces cost ? (   )

7. Mr. Brown is 56 years old, Mr. Green is 49 years old, and Mr. White is 38 years old. How old was Mr. Brown when Mr. White was born ? (   )

8. 1972 was a leap year. How many months were in that year ? (   )

9. Jack Brown has 3 brothers and 2 sisters. George Smith has 2 sisters. How many children are there in the Brown Family ? (   )

10. The bus fare to town is 8p. The buses run every 10 minutes, starting at 6.00 o'clock. How long will I have to wait for a bus if I arrive at the bus stop at 2 mins. after 6.45 ? (   )

EXERCISE 28

Underline the correct answer in the brackets.

Jane is absent from school more often than Julia.
Julia is absent more than Joan.

1. Who misses most lessons ? (Jane Julia Joan).

Sunday was wetter than Monday but sunnier than Saturday.

2. Which was the wettest day ? (Saturday Sunday Monday).

A man cycled from A to D. Soon after passing L he came to P, which was half way on his journey.

3. Which place is nearest to D ? (L P A)

4. Which is the longest distance ? (A to L, P to D, L to P)

Harry lives at No. 39 in a street in which the odd numbers are on one side. Jack lives at No. 43 which is two houses South of him. Tom lives four houses North of him.

5. What is the number of Tom's house ? (47 31 39 37 33 41 43 45 35)

Five cars took part in a race. The Morris beat the Vauxhall, but could not overtake the Singer. The Jowett beat the Singer, but could not overtake the Austin.

6. Which car was third ? (Morris Jowett Austin Singer Vauxhall).

Five boys go to the cinema together. When they sat down, John had one boy on his left and the others on his right. Maurice had one boy on his right and the others on his left. Sam sat on John's right and Victor on Maurice's right.

7. Which two boys were farthest apart ? (Sam Maurice John Victor Harry).

EXERCISE 29

These are figures and letters in steps with some steps missing. Can you put in the spaces the step that has been missed? You will notice that the steps are not in single jumps this time. Here is the alphabet to help you.

A B C D E F G H I J K L M N O P Q R S T U V W X Y Z

1.	A	C	E	G	I	......
2.	J	L	N	P	R	......
3.	Z	X	V	T	R	......
4.	1	3	5	7	9	......
5.	6	8	10	12	14	......
6.	15	17	19	21	23	......
7.	O	M	K	I	G	......
8.	g	i	k	m	o	......
9.	1a	2c	3e	4g	5i	......
10.	Hh	Jj	Ll	Nn	Pp	......
11.	E	G	......	K	M	O
12.	5	......	9	11	13	15
13.	U	S	Q	......	M	K
14.	14	16	18	20	......	24
15.	1b	2d	......	4h	5j	6l
16.	16	......	12	10	8	6
17.	29	27	25	......	21	19
18.	Dd	Ff	Hh.	Jj	......	Nn
19.	L	J	......	F	D	B
20.	4A	......	8C	10D	12E	14F

EXERCISE 30

You will see that the lines now have dots in them instead of words. Remember that

Cow : Calf :: Cat : Kitten means
Cow is to Calf as Cat is to Kitten.

Now see if you can fill in the spaces correctly.

1. Woman : Wife :: Man : ....
2. Sparrow : .... :: Man : House.
3. Wood : .... :: Bread : Knife.
4. Can : Will :: Cannot : ....
5. Smiles : Tears :: Happy : ....
6. Cows : Herd :: Wolves : ....
7. Leaf : .... :: Petal : Flower.
8. Wireless : .... :: Television : Look.
9. Prince : Princess :: Hero : ....
10. Ship : .... :: Train : Station.

The next lines are a little more difficult. ALL the words are in the lines and you must cross out one word in each bracket so that the line makes sense.

12. Coal is to (Black, Burn) as Snow is to (Ice, White)
13. Bottle is to (Baby, Milk) as Can is to (Tin, Petrol).
14. Eat : (Apple, Plate) :: Drink : (Cup, Mouth)
15. Well : (Water, Healthy) :: Mine : (Coal Yours)
16. Sea : (Look, Boat) :: Road : (Boat : Car)
17. Foot : (Leg : Shoe) :: Hand : (Finger, Arm)
18. Lamp : (Light, Oil) :: Fire : (Shoot, Heat)
19. Pen : (Write, Sheep) :: Chalk : (White, Draw)
20. Left : (Right, Write) :: Here : (Listen : There)

EXERCISE 31

Underline TWO words in the brackets which belong to the same group as the words before the brackets. Like this:—

Winter Spring (Water Autumn Flower Summer)

1. Happy glad (Joyous excited merry trembling)
2. Thin fat (young tall plump brainy)
3. Wife husband (son neighbour daughter friend)
4. Wet dry (windy foggy rusty smooth)
5. Bad good (careless tiny yesterday careful)
6. Milk cocoa (coffee soup gravy tea)
7. Wood timber (coal petrol logs sticks)
8. Wool cotton (silk worm nylon string)
9. Spoon knife (saucepan fork basin scissors)
10. March walk (run jump stagger limp)
11. White green (red blue shade tint)
12. Violin flute (organ recorder piano mouthorgan)
13. Box case (wood tub tank iron)
14. Wild savage (untamed animal wolf ferocious)
15. I me (you my them mine)
16. Witch wizard (fairy magician pantomime play)
17. Coach car (carriage lorry ambulance cart)
18. Duke lord (lady woman count numbers)
19. Love tenderness (affection home kindness ambulance)
20. Ring tinkle (clang orange peal wedding)

EXERCISE 32

In this exercise the questions are slightly harder. You should again choose the word, or group of words, in the brackets which make the sentence true. This time you must draw a ring round the part you choose.

1. Money always gives us (friends wealth happiness health).
2. Meals always give us (indigestion food manners company).
3. Doors are always (wooden hinged movable draughty).
4. Boys are always (human energetic truthful clean).
5. Tools are always (breaking metal wooden useful)
6. China is always (painted white brittle transparent).
7. Containers are always (receptacles round cardboard breakable).
8. A man is always a (husband descendant destroyer hunter).
9. A man-of-war is always a (soldier battleship crusader destroyer).
10. A miser is always (covetous prodigal old rude).
11. A mechanic is always (left-handed dirty expensive clever with tools).
12. An angler always has (two sides a point a fishing line a straight line).
13. A cousin always has a (father cousin sister brother).
14. Peal is always a (skin noise mountain town).
15. A lake always has (islands fish banks mud).
16. A mine always has (coal gold a shaft oil).
17. A dream is usually (pleasant frightening pretty sweet).
18. Sleep is always (fattening refreshing tiring tiresome).
19. Television is always (audible visual expensive cheap).
20. Fences are always (wooden metallic boundaries stone).

EXERCISE 33

A B C D E F G H I J K L M N O P Q R S T U V W X Y Z

1. Make a word with the letters which are in every one of these words:
   TELLING LISTEN TITLE LATER ....

2. How many of these words could be written by only using four letters of the alphabet for the word ?
   DEALER RALLY MUDDLE MEDDLE ....

3. If all the vowels were taken out of the alphabet, which would then be be the 12th letter ? ....

4. If the letters in the second half of the alphabet were put in order under the letters in the first half, which letter would be over Y ? ....

5. Which letter would be over P ? ....

6. Which letter would be under B ? ....

7. Which letter would be under H ? ....

8. Two letters in the word ABOUT are not in alphabetical order. Cross out the first of these letters.

9. If A comes before D, and L comes before H, write YES. It not, write NO. ....

10. Which is the second letter of the alphabet which would look the same if seen through a mirror ? ....

Here is a list of words. If a word has the letters I and E in it, put 1 in the bracket. If it has E and not I, put 2 in the bracket. If it has E and A, put 3 in the bracket. If it has two Ts, put 4 in the bracket. If it has D and E put 5 in the bracket. There may be some words with more than one figure in the bracket.

11. PAINTER ( )
12. DADDY ( )
13. PATTING ( )
14. TRUSTY ( )
15. TOPPLE ( )
16. TRADER ( )
17. LADDER ( )
18. PENCIL ( )
19. KNEELS ( )
20. LEANS ( )

EXERCISE 34

Many shopkeepers use code letters when they put the price on the articles they have for sale. I expect you have seen their labels with letters instead of figures for the price of something you have bought. This is the way they remember the code—a shopkeeper chooses a word or two words like this :

BROWN FACES — he then puts figures to the letters like this 1 2 3 4 5 6 7 8 9 0

When he wants to price anything at £1.46, he writes B.WF, because in his code B is the first letter, W is the 4th letter and F is the 6th.

Using this code, can you write out what the goods cost which are marked:—

1. B.OF	2. R.NE	3. A.BS ....
4. BE.BB	5. O.FS	6. WE.NS ....
7. B.AC	8. B.AN	9. O.NA ....
	10. OC.WS	

How would a shopkeeper mark articles worth:—

11. £1.79	12. £2.84	13. £1.82 ....
14. £19.20	15. £2.37	16. £3.56 ....
17. £5.29	18. £4.37	19. 89p ....
	20. £12.60	

How much would a shopkeeper lose if he marked:—

21. A coat for £O.NF instead of £O.FN ? ....
22. A hat for £B.OF instead of £B.FO ? ....
23. A suit for £BF.AS instead of £BA.FS ? ....
24. Trousers for £R.RN instead of £R.NR ? ....
25. A pullover for £O.WN instead of £W.ON ? ....

EXERCISE 35

Put a tick in front of the best reason.

1. We pay rates and taxes so that
   - (a) we shall have less money for pleasure.
   - (b) public services can be maintained.
   - (c) the tax collectors can have employment.
2. Hospitals are available to the people because
   - (a) the sick need care and treatment.
   - (b) visitors can take flowers to the patients.
   - (c) nurses must have somewhere to live.
3. We have furniture in our homes because
   - (a) we want to use up timber.
   - (b) we need it for comfort and use.
   - (c) we want to fill the rooms.
4. Tables have legs so that
   - (a) we are more comfortable when using a table.
   - (b) they can move about.
   - (c) we can polish them regularly.
5. Petrol is used for cars because
   - (a) garages have petrol pumps.
   - (b) it has a smell we associate with cars.
   - (c) it is the most satisfactory fuel for cars.
6. A judge wears a wig.
   - (a) as a symbol of his office.
   - (b) to keep the draught from his neck.
   - (c) because some judges are old and bald.
7. We use refrigerators
   - (a) to make the kitchen look tidy.
   - (b) to keep food fresh.
   - (c) to consume electricity.
8. We have chimneys to houses
   - (a) so that we can fasten television aerials to them.
   - (b) to carry away the smoke from fires.
   - (c) to provide the sweeps with work.
9. Station platforms are raised above the lines so that
   - (a) people can fall off them.
   - (b) they are level with the waiting room.
   - (c) they are level with the carriage doors.
10. People read books
    - (a) for information and entertainment.
    - (b) because we have public libraries.
    - (c) because they are printed in black and white.

EXERCISE 36

Can you put letters where there are dots and so make a good sentence ? Three dots represent a letter and the last dot in each sentence is the full stop.

1. I am a cat. I have two e...e... and a ...os... .
2. I am a tree. I have a tr......... and ...oo...s.
3. I am a car. I have four ......ee...s and a ...rive... .
4. I am a house. I have a ......of and a ...oo... .
5. I am an apple. I have a...tal... and p......s.
6. I am a boy. I have brown ...a...r and white ...e...t... .
7. I am a lion. I have a long ...a...e and sharp ...l...ws.
8. I am a mouse. I eat ...rum...s and I do not like ......ap... .
9. I am an orange. I have ......ice and ...eel.
10. I am a book. I have ......ges and l......te...s.
11. I am a teapot. I have a h......d...... and a sp......t.
12. I am a hand. I have a th......... and n.........s.
13. I am a hospital. I have d......t......s and n......s...s.
14. I am a house. I have w.........o...s and a c......m......y.
15. I am a motor car wheel. I have ....k...s and a ......r...
16. I am a garden. I have w......ds and ...l...w...rs.
17. I am a dairyman. I deliver ....k and ......gs.
18. I am a train. I carry g......ds and ...e...p...e.
19. I am a door. I ...p...n and ...l...s... .
20. I am the calendar. I show ... o...t...s and ...a...es.

EXERCISE 37

In this exercise you should put the things mentioned in order of size. Put 1 after the biggest, 2 after the next to the biggest and so on down to the smallest.

1. elephant ( ) cow ( ) mouse ( ) dog ( ) ant ( )
2. kennel ( ) mansion ( ) hut ( ) house ( ) bungalow ( )
3. tree ( ) trunk ( ) branch (3) twig ( ) leaf ( )
4. ambulance ( ) coach ( ) pram ( ) car ( ) moped ( )
5. book ( ) letter ( ) sentence ( ) word ( ) chapter ( )
6. pea ( ) football (1) golf ball ( ) orange ( ) grape ( )
7. 26 ( ) 62 ( ) 22 ( ) 32 ( ) 36 ( )
8. sun ( ) candle ( ) spark ( ) headlamp ( ) sidelamp ( )
9. eggcup ( ) basin ( ) cup ( ) milkjug ( ) bucket ( )
10. armchair ( ) settee ( ) stool ( ) chair ( ) desk ( )
11. overcoat ( ) cuff ( ) jacket ( ) waistcoat ( ) collar ( )
12. herring ( ) sardine ( ) cod ( ) whale ( ) shrimp ( )
13. nail ( ) needle ( ) skewer ( ) tent peg ( ) pin ( )
14. ocean ( ) puddle ( ) pond ( ) lake ( ) sea ( )
15. tree ( ) bush ( ) wood ( ) forest ( ) sapling ( )
16. rose ( ) violet ( ) petal ( ) lupin ( ) primrose ( )
17. field ( ) garden ( ) lawn ( ) farm ( ) prairie ( )
18. river ( ) trickle ( ) stream ( ) drop ( ) flood ( )
19. saucer ( ) teaplate ( ) soup plate ( ) tray ( ) table ( )
20. window ( ) porthole ( ) eyeglass ( ) windscreen ( ) spectacles ( )

EXERCISE 38

Put a number 1 in front of the first in order, number 2 in front of the second in order, and so on.

1. When we went to the seaside we

   ( ) packed our cases
   ( ) returned last Saturday
   ( ) got into the taxi to go away
   ( ) bought our tickets
   ( ) travelled to Southend

2. When we bought our house we

   ( ) planted an apple tree
   ( ) picked the apples
   ( ) dug the garden for a tree
   ( ) watched the blossoms fall
   ( ) made an apple pie.

3. To write a letter you should

   ( ) sit down and pick up the pen
   ( ) seal the envelope
   ( ) get some paper, pen and ink
   ( ) dip the pen in the ink
   ( ) put down the pen

4. To build a house you

   ( ) put the roof on
   ( ) buy the bricks
   ( ) dig the foundations
   ( ) mix the mortar
   ( ) build the walls

5. When we cross the road we

   ( ) look left
   ( ) look right again
   ( ) walk to a crossing
   ( ) look right
   ( ) stop at the pavement edge

6. When someone goes home he

   ( ) opens the front door
   ( ) puts the key in the lock
   ( ) opens the garden gate
   ( ) turns the key
   ( ) walks to the house

EXERCISE 39

This is the plan of the ground floor of a house. The arrow points to the North.

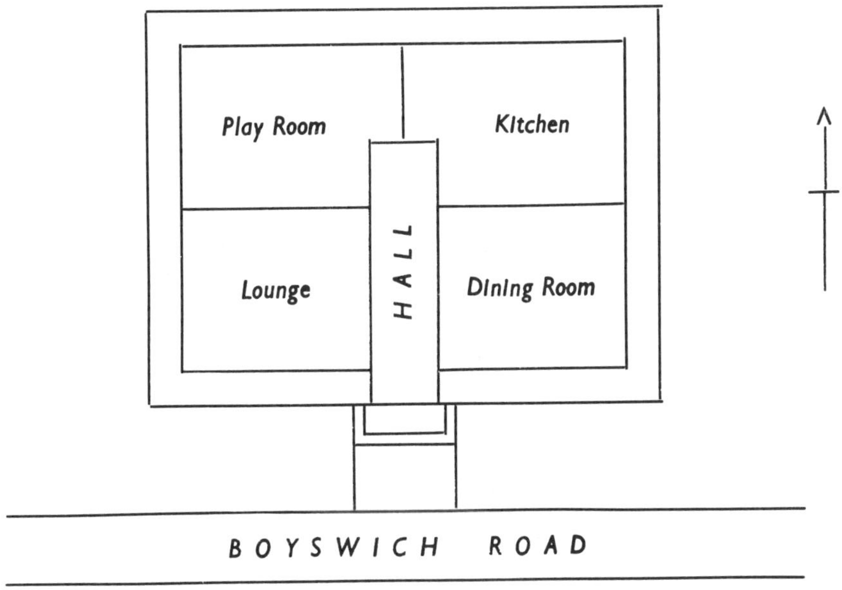

Cross out the words in the brackets you do not need.

1. The house is on the (North South East West) side of the road.
2. Boyswich Road runs from (West to East North to South).
3. The front of the house faces (North South East West)
4. The (kitchen lounge playroom) gets the morning sun.
5. The (lounge playroom kitchen) gets the midday sun.
6. The (lounge dining room kitchen) gets the evening sun.
7. I planted flowers which liked plenty of sun under the windows of the (lounge kitchen playroom).
8. The cold North wind blows on the (Kitchen lounge dining room).
9. The (morning midday evening) sun shines on the front door.
10. Only the (North South East West) wind blows directly into the hall.

EXERCISE 40

You know the signs used in number work, don't you ? They are :— + Add, − Take away, ÷ Divide, × Multiply.

In these sums some signs are missing. Can you put them in ? Put an ' add ' or ' take away ' sign over the dots.

(1) (5 + 3) ... 4 = 4 (2) (6 − 4) ... 5 = 7 (3) (10 − 3)... 4 = 11
(4) (8 + 4) ... 4 = 16 (5) (3 ... 7) − 6 = 4 (6) (22 − 17) ... 6 = 11
(7) (27 ... 2) − 10 = 19 (8) (37 ... 7) − 20 = 24 (9) (41 + 7) ... 6 = 54
(10) (50 ... 5) + 5 = 60

Now put the ' divide ' or ' multiply ' sign over the dots.

(11) (6 ÷ 3) ... 6 = 12 (12) (6 × 5) ... 10 = 3 (13) (21 ... 7) × 2 = 6
(14) (12 ... 2) ÷ 6 = 4 (15) (60 ... 5) ÷ 6 = 2 (16) (6 ... 4) × 2 = 48
(17) (27 ... 3) × 4 = 36 (18) (56 ... 7) ... 2 = 4 (19) (5 ... 2) ... 3 = 30
(20) (66 ... 11) ... 3 = 2

Now put in any of the four signs which are missing.

(21) (12 ÷ 6) ... 5 = 7 (22) (6 ... 3) × 2 = 18 (23) (16 ... 2) ÷ 9 = 2
(24) (7 ... 7) + 2 = 51 (25) (6 ... 4) ... 12 = 2 (26) (24 ... 6) ... 5 = 6
(27) (7 ... 5) ... 6 = 18 (28) (30 ... 2) ... 3 = 5 (29) (8 ... 4) ... 6 = 24
(30) (18 ... 6) ... 4 = 6

Put in the missing figure where there is a dot.

(31)
$$\begin{array}{r} .\ .\ 5 \\ \times\quad 7 \\ \hline 1\ 6\ 4\ 5 \\ \hline \end{array}$$

(32)
$$\begin{array}{r} 6\,\overline{)\ .\ 9\ .\ 4} \\ 3\ 1\ 9 \\ \hline \end{array}$$

(33)
$$\begin{array}{r} 8\,\overline{)\ 2\ .\ 6\ .} \\ 3\ 3\ 3 \\ \hline \end{array}$$

(34)
$$\begin{array}{r} 6\ .\ 7 \\ \times\quad . \\ \hline .\ .\ 5\ 9 \\ \hline \end{array}$$

(35)
$$\begin{array}{r} 2\ .\ 2\ . \\ \times\quad 8 \\ \hline 2\ .\ 8\ 2\ 4 \\ \hline \end{array}$$

(36)
$$\begin{array}{r} 7\ .\ 2\ . \\ \times\quad . \\ \hline 3\ 7\ 6\ 3\ 0 \\ \hline \end{array}$$

EXERCISE 41

Underline the correct words in the brackets.

1. My brother would be my (father's brother, father's father, mother's son, mother's father).
2. My uncle would be my (father's son, mother's son, father's brother, mother's father).
3. My nephew would be my (sister's son, father's son, sister's husband, wife's brother).
4. My cousin would be the son of my (mother's mother, mother's father, mother's brother, sister).
5. My niece would be my (mother's daughter, father's sister, sister's daughter, brother's wife).
6. My uncle would be my (sister's husband, mother's son, mother's brother, mother's father).
7. My grandfather would be my (father's father, mother's brother, sister's uncle, son's father).
8. My grandmother would be my (sister's mother, mother's mother, mother's sister, wife's daughter).
9. My aunt would be my (father's mother, daughter's mother, father's sister, brother's wife).
10. My cousin would be the daughter of my (father's mother, daughter's son, son's daughter, father's sister).

Underline the word in brackets which is the correct answer :—

11. The father of my mother is my (uncle, nephew, grandfather, cousin).
12. The sister of my mother is my (niece, aunt, grandmother, daughter).
13. The daughter of my father is my (aunt, cousin, niece, sister).
14. The son of my brother is my (cousin, uncle, nephew, grandfather).
15. The daughter of my brother is my (niece, cousin, aunt, sister).
16. The child of my father's sister is my (aunt, niece, cousin, nephew).
17. The mother of my father is my (aunt, niece, wife, grandmother).
18. The wife of my uncle is my (niece, aunt, cousin, sister).
19. The husband of my aunt is my (brother, cousin uncle).
20. My female parent is my (aunt, mother, sister, cousin).

EXERCISE 42

Complete each line with letters, numbers, or numbers and letters.

1.	A	D	G	J	M	....
2.	K	N	Q	T	W	....
3.	1	4	7	10	13	....
4.	7	11	15	19	23	....
5.	T	Q	N	K	H	....
6.	h	k	n	q	t	....
7.	AB	CD	EF	GH	IJ	....
8.	Aa	Ee	Ii	Mm	Qq	....
9.	B	BB	....	BBBB	....	BBBBBB
10.	a	aA	aAa	aAaA	....	aAaAaA
11.	$\frac{1}{2}$	1	$1\frac{1}{2}$	....	$2\frac{1}{2}$	3
12.	2	5	8	11	......	17
13.	A	B	A	C	A	......
14.	3	6	9	12	......	18
15.	1a2	3b4	....	7d8	9e10	11f12
16.	p	pa	......	pc	pd	pe
17.	$\frac{1}{2}$	$\frac{3}{4}$	1	$1\frac{1}{4}$	......	$1\frac{3}{4}$
18.	1/2	......	1/4	1/5	1/6	1/7
19.	ABC	BCD	CDE	......	EFG	FGH
20.	3	6	12	24	......	96

EXERCISE 43

Can you complete the lines correctly by filling the space that has been left ?

1. 2 is to $\frac{1}{2}$ as 4 is to ....
2. Now is to When as Here is to ....
3. Come is to .... as Go is to Depart.
4. Sword is to .... as Horse is to Animal.
5. Coal is to Smoke as Water is to ....
6. Cage : Animal :: .... : Prisoner.
7. Monastery : Monk :: .... : Nun.
8. Ally : Friendly :: Enemy : ....
9. Diamond : Gem :: Iron : ....
10. Wealth : Plenty :: Poverty : ....

In the next lines put a line under the part of each bracket which will make the whole line sensible.

11. Pine : (Sulk, Tree, Sorrow) :: Rose : (Up, Lifted, Flower)
12. 8 : (10. 6, 5) :: 12 : (16, 14. 7)
13. A : (B, Z, F) :: Start : (Begin, Run, Finish)
14. Hide : (Bury, Seek, Wallet) :: Fur : (Tree, Animal, Coat)
15. Flour : (Corn, Eggs, Baker) :: Flower : (Petal Stem, Florist).
16. Kernel : (Officer, Nut, Eat) :: Stone : (Weight, Brick, Plum).
17. Whale : (Sea, Blubber, Mammal) :: Greece : (Oil, Fat, Country).
18. Quay : (Lock, Ship, Answer) :: Platform : (Concert, Train, Ticket).
19. Pipe : (Mouth, Drain, Gas) :: Wire : (Telegram, Fence, Electricity)
20. Kid : (Goat, Baby, Glove) :: Cygnet : (Ring, Swan, Initials).

EXERCISE 44

Underline the two words in the brackets which are similar to the words at the beginning of each line. Like this :—

Warm, hot, frigid, (dry, tepid, chilly, wet)

1. Green purple orange (apple mauve blonde paint)
2. Modern new latest (novel ancient history recent)
3. Bitter tasteless sweet (toffee sour water tart)
4. Weak feeble lame (crippled hospital wound maimed)
5. Wet damp soaked (drenched slippery dissolved dead)
6. Affectionate loving likeable (heart wife devoted tender)
7. Plentiful teeming fruitful (prolific people fold glut)
8. Cheese butter milk (curds spider whey tuffet)
9. Strict stern firm (solid despotic sure harsh)
10. Cotton silk nylon (stocking wool fur shoes)
11. King queen president (ruler pencil dictator letter)
12. Large huge immense (gross gigantic tough rough)
13. Nail pin screw (peg skewer meat hammer)
14. Lawyer judge advocate (solicitor policeman gaoler attorney)
15. Weep cry sob (blubber whale mourn try)
16. Beef mutton pork (dinner veal lunch venison)
17. Sword revolver spear (tank sabre rapier fighter)
18. Boy youth baby (cygnet cub woman father)
19. Irish Welsh English (Holland Dutch Spain French)
20. Wire rope string (cable telephone hawser cart)

EXERCISE 45

In this exercise you should underline one of the words in the brackets which will complete the sentence and make it a true one.

Example :— Balloons, oranges and balls are all (juicy coloured round big).

You will see that round is the only word in the brackets which is correct for all the things mentioned.

1. Cats, dogs and rabbits all have (feet nests masters chains).
2. Cars, buses and bicycles all have (roofs windows seats engines).
3. Boys, girls and babies all have (teeth sisters shoes necks).
4. Mirrors, windows and lamps all have (wood locks glass iron).
5. Books, newspapers and comics all have (blue covers maps printing pictures).
6. Trees, bushes and plants all have (berries roots branches acorns).
7. Shoes, boots and sandals all have (laces soles straps rubber-heels).
8. Cows, sheep and dogs all eat (hay meat food fish).
9. Men, boys and girls are all (tall thin people healthy).
10. Tables chairs and stools all have (legs seats drawers cushions).
11. Bungalows, castles and houses all have (gardens gas walls porches).
12. Babies, puppies and kittens all grow (bigger smaller thinner shorter).
13. Cars, buses and aeroplanes all go (upward downward forward backward).
14. Apples, strawberries and plums all have (pips stones stalks peel).
15. Ovens, houses and garages all have (heat doors windows roofs).
16. Bottles, jugs and babies all have (milk necks handles shape).
17. Temples, churches and mosques all have (bishops services spires clocks).
18. Electricity, gas and water all give (light power smells shocks).
19. Molars, fangs and incisors are all (weapons teeth frightening fattening).
20. Frames, boundaries and margins are all (boarders wooden outer edges insides).

EXERCISE 46

In the next five questions you should put the words in each line in alphabetical order and then write the word which is required.

1. BIRD DONKEY ASS HORSE COW
   Which would be the first word ? ....
2. BABE BABY BABIES BABBLE BABBLING
   Which would be the first word ? ....
3. TOWN TOLL TOMATO TOES TONE
   Which would be the last word ? ....
4. ABLE ABSENT ABOUT ABAFT ABACK
   Which would be the last word ? ....
5. COFFEE CAMP CANE CORN CEREAL
   Which would be the middle word ? ....

In the next five questions you should change the first word into the third word by replacing one letter at each step, and put in the middle word.

Example :— YEAR TEAR TEAS

You will see in the example that the ' Y ' in the first word is changed to 'T' to make TEAR and then the ' R ' is changed to ' S '.

6. MEAN .... MELT   7. WASH .... LAST

8. MICE .... NINE   9. PIGS .... FAGS

10. NAME .... SOME

The next five questions have two steps missing:

11. LINE .... FIRE .... MITE
12. LIST .... LOSE .... MOPE
13. COAT .... COOL .... FOOT
14. DANGER .... RINGER .... RINSED
15. TRUCK .... TRACE .... GRADE
16. If all the vowels in this sentence were crossed out, how many letters would remain ? ......

Can you put the missing vowels into these sentences ? The question mark represents the same consonant in all the sentences.

17. ?H... GR...P... V...N... ...S ... ...S...F...L PL...NT
18. L...??L... D...GS C...N ......? L...RG... P......C...S ...F M......?
19. BR...SH ?......?H ...ND C...MB H......R ...V...RY N...GH?
20. ?H...? ...S N...? ?H... ?...M... ?... ?R...V...L

EXERCISE 47

Here is another form of code—the ' BOX ' type.

	1	2	3	4	5	6
J	B	O	S	L	I	T
K	G	D	A	Y	M	R
P	H	V	C	E	F	N

Instead of writing the letter B, I write J1, because the letter B is in the 1st. square of row J. Now try to read my sentences and answer ' YES ' or ' NO '.

1. P3 K3 P6 K2 J2 K1 J3 J1 J5 J6 P4

   ... ...

2. K2 J2 P4 J3 K3 J1 J5 K6 K2 J3 J5 P6 K1

   ... ...

3. K3 K6 P4 J4 P4 K3 P2 P4 J3 K1 K6 P4 P4 P6

   ... ...

4. J5 J3 P4 P2 P4 K6 K4 K2 K3 K4 J3 J6 J2 K6 K5 K4

   ... ...

   ....

5. J1 J2 K4 J3 K3 K6 P4 J3 J2 K5 P4 J6 J5 K5 P4 J3

   ... ...

   J3 P1 K3 J1 J1 K4

   ... ...

Now write these sentences in the same code :—

6. C O M E T O T E A

   ... ...

7. I L O V E M Y M O T H E R

   ... ...

8. C A L L F O R M E T H I S

   ... ...

   E V E N I N G

   ... ...

9. T E L L M E T H E D A T E

   ... ...

10. M O N D A Y I S B E F O R E F R I D A Y

    ... ...

EXERCISE 48

Here are some jumbled sentences. Each sentence is printed twice. If you cross out some words in A you will get a sensible sentence. If you cross out other words in B you will get another sentence. All the words are in their right order and no words need be added.

1. (A) Mary is a John is a boy girl.
   (B) Mary is a John is a boy girl.
2. (A) Cats like I like milk you very and meat much.
   (B) Cats like I like milk you very and meat much.
3. (A) Can you dogs can read climb a trees book.
   (B) Can you dogs can read climb a trees book.
4. (A) The rain the day was cold was not sunny.
   (B) The rain the day was cold was not sunny.
5. (A) Mother dad cooked the grew the dinner cabbages.
   (B) Mother dad cooked the grew the dinner cabbages.
6. (A) The car roofs was in the were blown off street.
   (B) The car roofs was in the were blown off street.
7. (A) Pour some milk people like into the cocoa cup.
   (B) Pour some milk people like into the cocoa cup.
8. (A) Look the car is coming both ways towards you along the road.
   (B) Look the car is coming both ways towards you along the road.
9. (A) Stop at the pick up your corner pen.
   (B) Stop at the pick up your corner pen.
10. (A) Each boy has many dogs are two brown eyes.
    (B) Each boy has many dogs are two brown eyes.
11. (A) Sometimes kittens have cats have cats kittens for mothers.
    (B) Sometimes kittens have cats have cats kittens for mothers.
12. (A) Cheese we is have made cheese for supper from milk.
    (B) Cheese we is have made cheese for supper from milk.

EXERCISE 49

In each question put the words in order in your mind, then underline the middle one of your order. You must first decide on what your order is going to be based—speed, size, time, etc.

1. dinner lunch supper breakfast tea
2. kitchen bedroom roof cellar attic
3. boy youth baby man old-man
4. crawl limp gallop run walk
5. 216 612 261 126 162
6. A E D C B
7. Thursday Wednesday Monday Tuesday Friday
8. August May July June April
9. cream grass milk cow butter
10. cord thread cotton rope string
11. pencil splinter pole match trunk
12. aeroplane bicycle scooter car train
13. soil slime mud rock water
14. road street highway track gardenpath
15. frozen warm cold hot boiling
16. January 26th. May 21st. April 9th. August 10th. July 17th.
17. writing stamp postbox postman reading
18. jam fruit blossom buds tarts
19. North-West West North South-West South
20. 13.15 hrs 22.45 hrs 17.10 hrs 14.18 hrs 15.16 hrs

EXERCISE 50

Here is the plan of the main roads of a village. The homes of some of the children are marked.

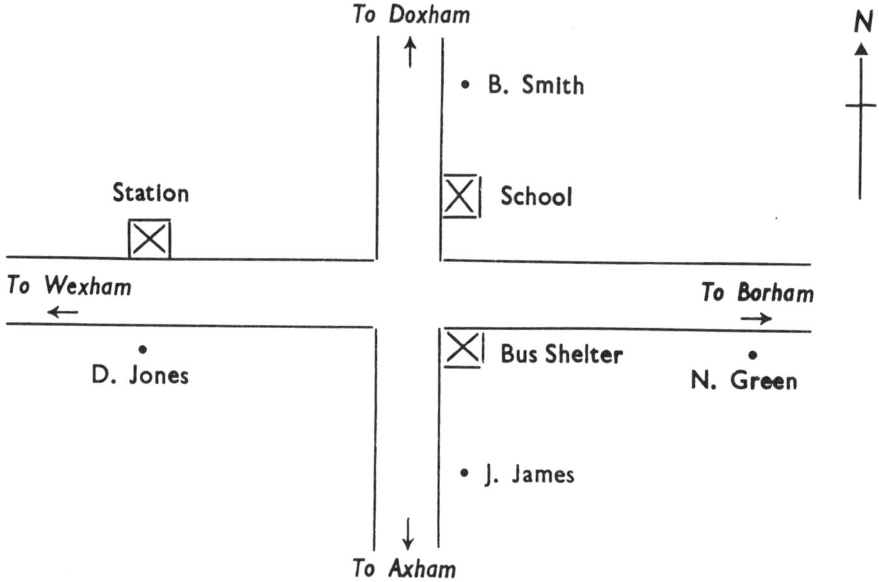

1. Nancy Green lives ...... of the school, so when she goes to school in the morning the sun shines on her (back, face, side).
2. Billy Smith goes ...... and then ...... to the station.
3. Dick Jones has the sun on his (face, back, side) when he goes to catch the morning bus at the shelter.
4. The driver of the (morning, midday, evening) bus has the sun in his eyes when he is going to Wexham.
5. The cold North wind blows on Billy Smith's (side, face, back) when he goes to school.
6. The south bound bus (does, does not) pass the station.
7. The (left, right) hand seats are the sunniest in the midday bus from Borham to Wexham.
8. At dinner time one day there was a smash outside Joe James house. One driver said he was blinded by the sun. He was travelling towards (Axham, Borham, Doxham, Wexham).

EXERCISE 51

In these sums some of the figures have been missed out and a dot put in place of each figure. Look carefully at the sign which tells you the type of sum, and then put in the missing figures.

(1) 9 − . 8	(2) 1 5 − . 7	(3) 1 4 − 8 .	(4) 2 4 − . . 1 2	(5) 4 × . 2 0
(6) 1 2 × . 4 8	(7) 4 × . . 4 4	(8) 1 6 × . 4 8	(9) .) 2 7 9	(10) 3) 3 . 1 2
(11) 7) . 6 8	(12) 3) . 4 2 8	(13) . 1 − 1 8 6 .	(14) 6 2 − 3 . . 5	(15) 3 . 3 − . 4 6 1 0 .
(16) 1 . × 7 . . 5	(17) 4 1 1 − . . 2 4 5	(18) . 3 × . 1 . 7	(19) 5 . × 8 . . 0	(20) . . 9 × . 1 1 5 6
(21) 5 4 3 2 . . 9 7	(22) 4 4 1 . . 3 8 9	(23) 5 . . 3 2 1 9 8	(24) 5 . 2 2 3 5 1 0 9	
(25) 2 7 1 6 − 1 5 . 3 . . 1 .	(26) 3 . 4 2 − 1 2 . . . 9 1 9	(27) 4 2 . . − . . 3 4 1 8 9 5	(28) 6 2 1 2 − . . 4 9 2 8 . .	
(29) 2 1 6 4 3 2 5 6 . . . . 9 5 4 3	(30) 2 . 4 5 . 2 3 4 2 5 6 . 8 4 . 6	(31) 2 . 5 . × 7 1 . 4 . 2	(32) 1 . . . × 9 1 0 3 7 7	
(33) £ 6-70 − .-.. 3-85	(34) £ 5-30 − .-.. 2-61	(35) £ 12-.. − .-60 7-48	(36) £ 9-75 + .-.. 15-25	
(37) £ ..-35 × . 74-10	(38) £ 4) 9-36 .-.8	(39) £ 28-42 3.-7. + .6-.5 108-51	(40) £ ..-.. × 7 .25-33	

EXERCISE 52

In the house at the corner of the road lives Mr. Green and his wife. They have twin sons, Jack and James, and daughters Sally and June.

1. How many brothers has Jack ? ....
2. How many sisters has James ? ....
3. How many sisters has June ? ....
4. How many in the family ? ....
5. What is the name of Jack's mother ? ....

Mr. Page, his wife, and their children Paul, Susan and Moira, went to spend their holiday on a farm owned by George Whiting who had married Mr. Page's sister Mary.

6. What was Mary's full name ? ....
7. What was Moira's full name ? ....
8. How many nieces has Mr. Page ? ....
9. How many nieces has his sister ? ....
10. How any adults are mentioned ? ....

Here are the birth dates of a family. Study them and answer the questions. George Garside—3rd April, 1962. Mabel Garside—21st December, 1914. Mary Garside—14th September, 1941. Harry Garside—5th July, 1969. Jean Garside—27th October, 1964. Fred Garside—13th September, 1935. Samuel Garside—3rd June 1901. Teresa Garside—3rd April, 1962.

What are the Christian names of the

11. Grandmother.................
12. Grandfather ....
13. Mother ....
14. Father ....
15. Younger girl....................
16. Twins .... & ....
17. Elder girl ....
18. Younger boy ....
19. Youngest child ....
20. Oldest person ....

EXERCISE 53

In this exercise you will notice that the pairs of words follow a pattern. Each question has a different pattern.

Example :— fat—sat fit—sit fun—sun fin—(sin)

You will see that the letter ' f ' in the first word of each pair is changed to the letter ' s ' to make the second word. The correct answer in this example is the word ' sin ' in the brackets.

1. nice—mice neat—meat nine—mine nail—( ).
2. line—fine list—fist loot—foot last—( ).
3. bat—cat bone—( ) ball—call bode—code.
4. ten—men toss—moss tap—( ) tale—male.
5. sit—lit sap—lap said—( ) sip—lip.
6. ten—net bat—tab pan—nap won—( ).
7. pat—tap bin—( ) top—pot pal—lap.
8. lone—one cape—ape late—ate cant—( ).
9. bowl—( ) fort—for feet—fee cart—car.
10. slows—low shows—( ) shacks—hack stones—tone.
11. pin—pun tin—tun sin—sun bin—( ).
12. file—fool pile—( ) tile—tool wile—wool
13. strap—parts strop—ports straw—warts strops—( )
14. up—down high—low in—out far—( ).
15. to—tow so—sow lo—low no—( ).
16. Monday—Tuesday Friday—Saturday Sunday—Monday Thursday—( ).
17. cat—( ) dog—pup cow—calf hen—chick.
18. old—new fat—( ) sharp—blunt tall—short.
19. write—pen paint—( ) buy—money walk—legs.
20. steam—seam stolid—( ) blind—bind clamp—camp.

EXERCISE 54

In each line three of the things mentioned are included in the 'GROUP' name on that line. One is not in the Group. Draw a ring round the Group name and cross out the one not in the Group. Like this :

Cow (Animal) Sheep Pig ~~Herring~~

1. Rose Tulip Carrot Flower Pansy
2. Five Number One Few Six
3. London Bristol Cardiff Town Thames
4. Fire Table Furniture Chair Stool
5. Brass Iron Gold Metal Plastic
6. Dress Frock Jacket Ring Clothes
7. Road Avenue Street Footpath Highway
8. Robin Thrush Bird Sparrow Cat
9. Anne Name Ann Annie Aunty
10. Hours Ours Minutes Seconds Time
11. Baby Child Boy Girl Family
12. Nelson Drake Cook Sailor Soldier
13. Carrot Turnip Orange Potato Vegetable
14. Plum Rose Apple Fruit Pear
15. Oak Ash Elm Tree Rose
16. Square Round Thick Shape Oval
17. Oil Petrol Fuel Coal Soil
18. Fog Snow Steam Rain Weather
19. Black Colour Blue Red Pale
20. Man Woman Dog Girl People

EXERCISE 55

A B C D E F G H I J K L M
N O P Q R S T U V W X Y Z

In the above code you write the letter which is the partner (either above or below) instead of the real letter.

Example :— SAFETY would be written as FNSRGL

Now try putting these words in this code)—

1.	MUST	....	2.	RIVET	....
3.	NICELY	....	4.	STEW	....
5.	LAZY	....	6.	TUSK	....
7.	FULLY	....	8.	PAST	....
9.	NEAREST	....	10.	COVERED	....

Using the above code, what words do these letters stand for ?

11.	CVRPR	....	12.	EVQRF	....
13.	OBARF	....	14.	GRNCBG	....
15.	EBHAQ	....	16.	YRNFG	....
17.	TEBHC	....	18.	PYNJF	....
19.	ARIRE	....	20.	RKREPVFR	....

Now answer these questions. Each one has its own code.

21. If PYRE stands for POLE, what is PYRY ? ....
22. If LZXY stands for DAME, what is XZLZX ? ....
23. If BACON stands for TILER, what is CABBCO ? ....
24. If WOMAN stands for SHAWL, what is AMNNW ? ....
25. If YZZWP stands for REELS, what is WZPPZY ? ....
26. If PURSE is written as TLMOZ, how would SUPPER be written ? ....
27. If SEATS is written as PTRBP, how would TEASE be written ? ....
28. If DRAWER is written as PLUVAL, how would WARDER be written ? ....
29. If SHOULD is written as NMTRGE, how would DOLLS be written ? ....
30. If CUSTARD is written as LMNFBEC, how would STARDUST be written ? ....

EXERCISE 56

In these little stories you should choose the word you think is the best one out of each bracket. Cross out the other two.

Last summer John went to a farm in the country to (try spend get) his holiday. The (keeper policeman farmer) met him at the gate and took him (into near upon) the (house shed garage) to have his (sleep lessons dinner). After the meal he went with the farmer to the (city house stable) where they fed the (pigs, horses fish). They took their (tractor time chairs) to the (garden trees field) and brought back a load of (furniture hay trouble) to feed the (cows sheep pigs) before they were milked. The milk was put in large (cans sacks letters) which were collected by (boat lorry bicycle) and taken to the (mill dairy church). John was very (tired tall fresh) at the end of the day and soon went to (market school sleep) in the little (box room parcel) with the ivy round the (fire window floor). He dreamed that he was being (sunk chased tossed) in the air by a huge (bull hen donkey) with long sharp horns.

Once upon a (bus time boat) through a strange (country book idea) there (rowed rode road) some goodly knights and their (breath, path, meals) lay by a deep wood, where tangled briars grew very (thin weak thick) and strong, and tore the (paper envelopes flesh) of them that lost their way therein. And the leaves of the (books trees tables) that grew in the (library room wood) were very dark and (light heavy thick), so that no (ray electricity gas) of light came through the (ground moss branches) to lighten the (weight load gloom) and sadness. And as they (jumped passed swam) by that dark wood, one (night knight soldier) of those that rode, missing his (money dinner comrades), wandered far (apart away along) and (refused retired returned) to them no more ; and they, sorely grieving, rode on (beside with without) him, (keeping mourning refusing) him as (alive awake dead)

(from Three Men in a Boat)

EXERCISE 57

Here is the table of Roman numerals.

I	= 1	X	= 10	C	= 100	M	= 1000
II	= 2	XX	= 20	CC	= 200		
III	= 3	XXX	= 30	CCC	= 300		
IV	= 4	XL	= 40	CD	= 400		
V	= 5	L	= 50	D	= 500		
VI	= 6	LX	= 60	DC	= 600		
VII	= 7	LXX	= 70	DCC	= 700		
VIII	= 8	LXXX	= 80	DCCC	= 800		
IX	= 9	XC	= 90	CM	= 900		

To help you in these questions I will tell you that the Romans wrote their numbers as we do—thousands are written first; then hundreds; tens and then units. They did not use a 'nought' as we do.

For example:—506 would be written DVI. CIV = 104.

Now write these numbers in Roman numerals:

1. 22 .... 2. 37 .... 3. 45 .... 4. 91 ....
5. 49 .... 6. 69 .... 7. 101 .... 8. 304 ....
9. 505 .... 10. 401 .... 11. 566 .... 12. 709 ....
13. 1006 .... 14. 1505 .... 15. 999 .... 16. 1800 ....
17. 2002 .... 18. 555 .... 19. 2121 ....
20. 4444 ....

Now change these Roman numbers into ordinary numbers:

21. XVIII .... 22. XIX .... 23. XLIV ....
24. XXXVIII .... 25. LXIX .... 26. CIX ....
27. CDLV .... 28. MCMIX .... 29. MDIV ....
30. MCLV .... 31. CMXC .... 32. DCCLXX ....
33. XCIX ...... 34. DCCCI .... 35. CDXC ....
36. CXI .... 37. CCXXII .... 38. DLIV ....
39. MCMLXX .... 40. XXXIX ....

EXERCISE 58

This is a 'family tree', or to give it its full title, a GENEALOGICAL TABLE. Study it carefully and then answer the questions.

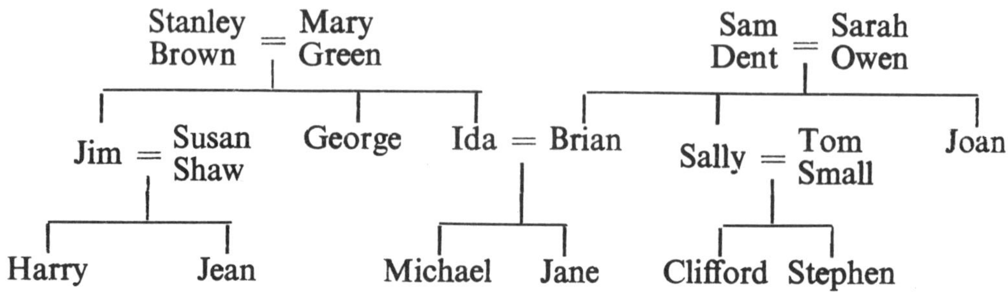

Give the surnames of the following people:—

1. Jean .... 2. Brian ....

3. Stephen .... 4. Sally ....

5. Joan .... 6. George ....

7. Michael .... 8. Jane ....

9. Harry .... 10. Ida ....

What relationship is :—

11. Susan to Jim ? .... 12. Michael to Jane ? ....

13. Sam to Brian ? .... 14. George to Mary ? ....

15. Tom to Sally ? .... 16. Jean to Michael ? ....

17. Brian to Clifford ? .... 18. Sally to Jane ? ....

19. Sam to Clifford ? .... 20. Jean to Mary ? ....

How many :—

21. Uncles has Michael ? ...... 22. Grandchildren has Mary ? ......

23. Daughters has Sam ? ...... 24. Cousins has Jane ? ......

25. Aunts has Michael ? ......

EXERCISE 59

Here is another exercise on word patterns which you will probably find a little harder. Put <u>two</u> correct words in the brackets.

1. ( )—teams stone—tones scamp—( ) scream—creams.
2. loot—tool live—( ) part—trap ( )—stop.
3. blouse—blood ( )—hood mouse—( ) rouse—rood.
4. tone—( ) rate—tare kale—lake ( )—lope.
5. slip—sludge ( )—drudge grip—( ) nip—nudge.

The next five questions have numbers to represent letters. In each question the number given for a letter doesn't change. In question 10 the answer should be numbers only.

6. 1234—leap 4231—peal 4221—( ) 4312—pale.
7. star—5678 tars—6785 rats—( ) stars—56785.
8. pine—2134 port—2567 rope—6524 tent—( ).
9. later—5ate6 mated—7ate9 mates—7ate8 slate—( ).
10. tipped—123ped padded—489ded puddle—pud967 paddle—( ).

Now try some patterns of three words.

11. pen—pens—opens range—ranges—( ) live—lives—olives.
12. ant—rant—grant aft—( )—graft ail—rail—grail.
13. tram—mart—smart pot—top—( ) pan—nap—snap.
14. pat—tap—( ) not—ton—tons ( )—nip—nips.
15. stop—tops—topped spot—( )—potted spit—pits—( ).
16. ( )—tone—stone art—( )—start rip—trip—( ).
17. in—( )—binds on—bond—( ) ( )—band—bands.
18. feat—feet—( ) meat—( )—melt ( )—peel—pelt.
19. much—( )—most ( )—better—best little—less—( ).
20. two—four—( ) three—( )—nine ( )—eight—twelve.

EXERCISE 60

Underline the word in each line which includes all the other words in that line. Like this :—

Walk run <u>move</u> jump crawl

1. Love hate anger feeling sympathy
2. Taste touch sense smell sight
3. Yew lime pear tree willow
4. Gas fuel petrol oil coal
5. Car bus tram cart vehicle
6. Diamond ruby gem emerald amethyst
7. House dwelling bungalow mansion cabin
8. Running walking swimming exercising skipping
9. Hour day month year time
10. Office factory building church garage
11. Wheat rye cereal barley oats
12. Good bad quality poor cheap
13. London Bristol Leeds City Liverpool
14. Knife fork spoon scissors cutlery
15. Wife relative sister aunt cousin
16. Time yesterday today evening tomorrow
17. Writing paper wrapping greaseproof wall
18. Mumps disease smallpox fever influenza
19. Tin metal brass iron steel
20. Hot temperature cold chilly warm

EXERCISE 61

In this exercise put a ring round the word in the brackets which does not apply to all the words before the brackets.

Example :— Babies, boys, girls (young (tall) children)

The word ' tall ' has a ring round it because babies, boys and girls are all young and children but not all tall.

1. Cheese nuts milk (soft, food, nourishing).
2. Cabbage lettuces sprouts (green, grow, cooked).
3 Iron wood brass tin (metals, useful, heavy).
4. Sideboard sofa chair stool (made, furniture, seats).
5. Cane raffia cotton (vegetable, pliable, white).
6. Teeth bone tusks (hard, pointed, parts of an animal).
7. Oil water petrol (wet, liquids, fuels).
8. Repay refer recent (verbs, words, pronounceable).
9. Books essays newspapers (read, bought, writing).
10. Laugh cry smile (visible, audible, emotional).

In the next questions cross out the word before the brackets which does not fit in with the words in the brackets.

Example :— ~~boys~~ girls maidens (females young growing).

The word ' boys ' is crossed out because although they could be young and growing they could not be females.

11. Weeds crops cereals (grow cultivated harvested).
12. Kettles basins jugs (utensils pottery containers).
13. Leg arm neck (limb bend jointed).
14. Entertainment tragedy wedding (pleasant happy enjoyable).
15. Cooker boiler baker (containers metal manufactured).
16. Tumbler pane teapot (glass breakable transparent).
17. Felony charity donation (good beneficial helpful).
18. Goose mongoose drake (bird feathers eats).
19. Siren hymn psalm (noise tune sung).
20. Pink rose blush (scent flower grows).

EXERCISE 62

In this exercise you have to find the code before you can answer the questions. You will see that numbers are placed over the words to represent the letters, but the groups of numbers are not over the correct words. Your first task is to get the correct groups of numbers in the right place. You should look for a clue in the relationship between the groups of numbers and the words. Perhaps there is a five lettered word and a five figured number, while all the others are four figured. Perhaps there is a word with a double letter in it, and a double number to match. There may also be a clue in the letters which begin or end the words. Figures in each group always stand for the same letters.

2 4 6 3	2 3 3 6	2 3 6 3	2 3 4 6	2 7 5 6
F E A T	F A T E	F E E T	F O R T	F E T E
______	______	______	______	______

Use this code to write the words for :—

1. 6345 .... 2. 2776 .... 3. 646635 ....

4. 57675 .... 5. 34635 ....

Here is a similar code problem.

6 5 2 7	7 5 2 6	6 5 7 5 8	7 5 2 1
M E T E R	T E A S	M E A T	T E A M
______	______	______	______

Use this code to write the words for :—

6. 8271 .... 7. 627758 .... 8. 21151 ....

9. 1752658 .... 10. 1726658 ....

Here is another similar code problem :—

1 2 7 6	3 2 7 6	8 7 4 5	1 5 7 6	8 2 7 6
B E A T	M O A T	B O A T	M A L E	G O A T
______	______	______	______	______

Using this code, write the words for these figures :—

11. 628762 .... 12. 176645 ....

13. 873326 .... 14. 874456 ....

15. 174426 ....

Here is another similar code problem :—

S NO W	S O UP	S O UL	S U N S	S L O W
1 2 4 6	1 4 3 1	1 3 2 7	1 6 2 7	1 2 4 5

Using this code, what words do these numbers represent ?

16. 15223.................... 17. 1262 .... 18. 16225 ....

19. 52261 .... 20. 5431 ....

Here is a similar code problem with signs instead of numbers.

SABLE	BALES	BLEAT	TABLE	BEATS
£@&$\frac{1}{2}$?	£$\frac{1}{2}$@$\frac{1}{4}$?	?@£&$\frac{1}{2}$	£&$\frac{1}{2}$@$\frac{1}{4}$	$\frac{1}{4}$@£&$\frac{1}{2}$

Using this code what words do the following stand for ?

21. £@££&$\frac{1}{2}$ .... 22. $\frac{1}{4}\frac{1}{2}$&&$\frac{1}{4}$@&$\frac{1}{2}$ ....

23. &@£$\frac{1}{2}$&? ....

24. &$\frac{1}{2}$@?$\frac{1}{2}$? .... 25. $\frac{1}{2}$@$\frac{1}{4}$@£&$\frac{1}{2}$ ....

Here is a similar code problem using letters instead of figures or signs.

SEVER	LOVES	LEVER	LOVER	ROVES
BACAT	TSCAO	BSCAO	BSCAT	OACAT
....	....	....	....	....

How would you write the following words in code ?

26. VEERS .... 27. LOSES ....

28. SOLVES .... 29. REVOLVER ....

39. RESERVE ....

EXERCISE 63

Here are some questions on the eight main points of the compass. You may make drawings if you wish on a piece of rough paper.

John leaves home and walks $\frac{1}{2}$ mile East to the Post Office. He then walks $\frac{1}{2}$ mile North to the Station.

1. What direction is his home from the Station ? ....
2. If he walks $\frac{1}{2}$ mile West from the Station to the School—how far is his home from the school as the crow flies ? ....
3. What direction is the Post Office from the Station ? ....
4. What direction is the Post Office from the School ? ....
5. I look in the mirror and see the setting sun behind me. In which direction am I looking ? ....

Here is a square room. The door is on the centre of the South side, and it opens into the room towards the East.

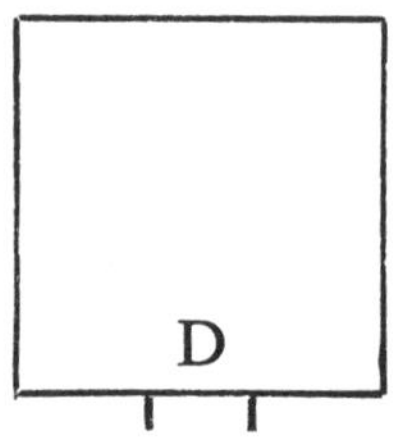

6. Put W for window in the centre of the East wall.
7. Put F for fireplace in the centre of the West wall.
8. Put T for television in the North-West corner.
9. Put R for radio in the corner behind the door.
10. Put S for shelf across the North-East corner.

Here are some letters to represent soldiers on parade. The arrow shows the North.

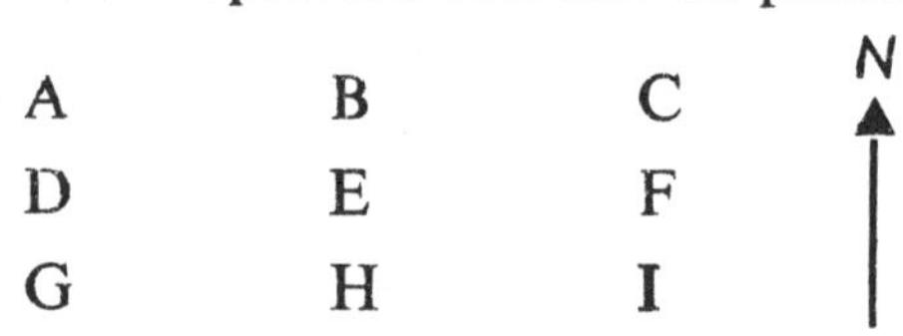

11. When they all face South, who is in the centre of the front row ?...........

12. " Right Turn !" the sergeant said, ... is now in the centre of the back row and they are all facing ....

13. When they face the North-West, who is the front man ? ....

14. Who can never be in the front row whichever way the group faces ?.........

15. Who can never be in the rear row whichever way the group faces ?.........

16. If a man could stand at the North Pole, which direction would he look to see the setting sun ? ....

17. If a man stands on the Equator, which direction should he look to see the rising sun ? ....

18. A man standing at the South Pole has his back to the North. He turns round and he now has his back to the ....

19. If I lie on my back with my feet towards the South, and point sideways with my left hand, in what direction am I pointing ? ....

20. If I stand on my head looking South, and point sideways with my left hand, in which direction am I pointing ? ....

EXERCISE 64

Jim is 7 years old and half as old as his brother Harry. Jack is two years younger than Jim and the same number of years older than Mary.

1. Who is the oldest child ?
   (Jim Mary Jack Harry)
2. Who is the youngest child ?
   (Jim Mary Jack Harry)
3. How old is Mary ?
   (1 2 3 4 5 6 7 8)
4. How old is Harry ?
   (7 8 9 10 11 12 13 14)
5. Harry has (1 2 3 4) brothers).

Here are some names from a school register, with birthdays.

Janet Jones 5th Nov. 1937. James Green 14th August, 1936. Harold Smith 27th July, 1936. Ann Smart 12th May, 1936. Mary Green, 16th Sept. 1941. Susan Grant, 15th July, 1936.

6. Who is the oldest child ? (Janet, James, Harold, Mary, Ann, Susan)
7. Who is the youngest child ?
   (Janet, James, Harold, Mary, Ann, Susan)
8. Is James older than his sister ? (yes, no).
9. (Mary, Ann, Susan) is the oldest girl.
10. Harold is (older, younger) than Susan.

In a cloak room there were six pegs with coats on them. Numbers 1, 3 and 5 were ladies coats, the rest were men's. Numbers 1 and 3 were grey, 2 and 5 were brown, the others were black. Numbers 3 and 5 and 6 were for short persons, the rest for tall persons.

11. The tall lady's grey coat was on peg (1, 2, 3, 4, 5, 6).
12. The short man's black coat was on peg (1, 2. 3, 4, 5, 6).

In a block of flats there are six families. The flats are numbered in the diagram. Can you put in the names ?

5	6
3	4
1	2

The Reeds live in an even number flat with the Grays below them. The Browns live opposite the Blacks, and Greens and Roses live opposite families with different initials. The Blacks live in an even number flat between two families.

EXERCISE 65

In each line there are two groups of words. Draw a line under each word in one group, and a ring round each word in the other group. Like this :

(Cow) Rose Tulip (Sheep) (Pig) Snowdrop

1. Big Great Small Large Tiny Little
2. Nice Spiteful Rude Pretty Nasty Pleasant
3. Oil Petrol Ash Sand Grease Grit
4. Father Friend Neighbour Teacher Mother Uncle
5. Red Rose Poppy Pink Carnation Scarlet
6. Brian Mary George Ann Susan Peter
7. Paper Box Postcard Case Trunk Cardboard
8. Horse Cow Calf Pony Donkey Bull
9. Road Street Cart Lane Car Train
10. Smile Scowl Laugh Frown Sneer Giggle
11. Forest Feather Wood Wool Tree Hair
12. Tin Brass String Rope Cord Iron
13. Teeth Wrist Hand Eyes Finger Mouth
14. Wool Needle Cotton Pin Silk Bodkin
15. Hit Stroke Knock Smack Soothe Fondle
16. Port Harbour Ship Dock Steamer Warship
17. Ball Jump Run Toy Walk Doll
18. Football Cricket Tennis Swimming Hockey Skating
19. Jack Coach Jill Cinderella Prince Water
20. Cry Weep Dear Costly Sob Cheap